Edition CG04
$2.95
(Group prices available)

Ralph Middlecamp

Introduction to Catholic Music Ministry

PASTORAL ARTS ASSOCIATES OF NORTH AMERICA
GLENDALE ¤ ARIZONA

First Printing: March, 1978
ISBN 0-89699-012-5
Edited and Designed by Dan F. Onley

Printed in the United States of America

I.
Being and Becoming
a Minister of Music

THE MINISTER OF MUSIC

A singing congregation breathes, speaks, moves, thinks and prays as one body. Like the Eucharist we celebrate, music is more than just a sign of our unity in the body of Christ — it is an experience of that unity. The role music is not merely that of expressing the words of the liturgy — music also communicates a dimension of meaning and feeling that cannot be done by words alone. If our worship is to speak to our whole selves, then good music is essential.

The minister of music, or "pastoral musician", is responsible for planning and leading the music in our celebrations. The primary duty of this person is to **lead the people in prayer through music.** This people requires people with special dedication and ability. They must be competent musicians as well as good group leaders. Simultaneously they are both musicians and ministers. Both elements are essential. Ministers of music need to be people who pray. In Christian worship, music is much more than an art. Music is a powerful sign which needs to be presided over by people who have a faith that gives it life.

AM I ONE?

Pastoral musicians sometimes become uneasy as I talk with them about the ministry that is theirs. Many musicians do not see themselves as "ministers." In case you have the same feeling, be assured at this early point that if you are "doing the music" at a mass on a regular basis, you either are a minister of music, or you should start becoming one. Your desire to become a minister is the necessary first step. In either case, this book is written for you as a first step forward in understanding and claiming your ministry in the Church.

BEING A MUSICIAN

Before you can lead music, you need to be a musician yourself. This book cannot make you that. It takes lessons, practice, experience and **more practice.** Musical ability is a skill that needs to be developed, regardless of the style of music you play. A guitarist with one year of experience should not assume to be qualified to lead music at Sunday Mass, nor should a person with only a few grades of piano lessons be playing organ at Mass.

This is not to say that our musicians have to be perfect, or that there is no place for beginners and students. Worship is an activity of humans, and humans make mistakes. The quest for perfection of skills must not overshadow the desire to simply pray, and to serve others who want to pray. However, music for worship, especially at parish Sunday celebrations, should be done by musicians who are competent, or else the resulting music will detract harmfully from the celebration. Sometimes no music at all is better than that which is done poorly.

In stating the case for competence strongly, I do not want to discourage beginners who do have something to offer. Celebrations for families and small groups and classes are possible times for beginners to share their talent in a very personal and understanding environment.

BEING A LEADER

As a minister of music, you are not just "doing" the music — you are leading people in music. The whole celebrating community needs to be led by a confident, strong, and loving person. How a song is introduced and led often can make the difference between a singing group and a silent one.

Often we assume that leadership is a gift with which people are born. Leadership, however, can be learned. Much of it is a matter of confidence and an ability to speak well. Confidence is rooted in a mix of experience and competence. You need to speak slowly enough and loudly enough to be heard by everyone. Without sounding like an unpleasant dictator, you must convey to everyone that you do expect them to sing with you.

Because of the leadership role of music ministry, I do not think that grade school children should lead music at Sunday Mass, for they simply do not have the skills to be leaders of an adult group. Placing children into this kind of situation has frequently given a bad name to liturgical folk music

KNOWING YOUR PEOPLE

A necessary quality of a good leader is a knowledge and understanding of the people who are being led. For a minister of music this understanding is necessary in making the judgements concerning the choice of music. It also affects how you relate to the whole group.

The first thing to learn about a group is its history. Find out the kinds of music and music experiences they have had. Find out what kinds of people and groups have led the music in the past. Knowing this history is essential preparation for leading effectively. Very bad experiences in the past will affect their responses and attitudes today. Very neutral experiences will usually have the same bad effect! Very good experiences also need to be taken into serious consideration, since no group could ever stand to move backward. In any case, you must be prepared for resistance, for strong expectations, for no expectations whatsoever.

The most important thing to know about a parish community, and also about specific groups (which tend to frequent certain Mass times, etc.), is where people's tastes and concerns are **right now.** You must be sensitive to the prevailing opinions, even if those opinions counter the direction in which you hope to lead the people. You must begin at the point where they are. You cannot lead people in prayer through music if they do not like what you are doing. There are many obvious ways to find out what they like and dislike. The smiles, scowls, and blank stares on various faces tell you something every Sunday. The comments you receive after Mass and during the week give you more direct feedback. Some of these comments will be unsolicited, and others you should seek out. You might consider a formal survey from time to time.

What people say they want now may not always be what is best for them. However, the prerequisite for leading them to something better is a sensitive understanding of their present reality. Every celebrating group can be more and do more if it has good leadership. Part of your ministry is to call people to grow. As you do so, remember that the Church is a living body and therefore grows slowly. Do not expect people to change overnight.

If it is evident that radical growth is needed in your parish, you may expect the process to take several years and that it necessarily involves all ministries in the worship experience. Being a minister of music puts you in contact with many people. As a minister, you must pay attention to these people and seek to serve them. This is not always easy. There is more to being a minister of music than liking to play music. You must like to work with people, and you must know how to do so.

OPENNESS

Part of your task in leading people in growth is paying attention to your own need for openness about music for worship. Many parish communities have been badly damaged by music-rooted hostilities. The organ and the guitar have become the symbols for a divisiveness that must be healed. You are entitled to your music preferences, but you must be careful to not allow these personal preferences to interfere with your ministry. In exercising your ministry, you must clearly show everyone your respect and appreciation for the great variety of styles and idioms of liturgical music.

LEADING THE PEOPLE IN MUSIC

Your actual manner and method of leading music depends on your ability and your personality. Other things that will affect your method include the physical arrangement of the church, the ability of the congregation and also the participation aid that is being used.

The key to leading music is **communication.** Speak loudly enough to be heard by everyone. Let your voice communicate a sincere interest in the people. Make eye contact. Within reason, let your whole body communicate — the sweep of your hands, the rhythm of your body, your nods and smiles.

Here is a series of suggestions about
leading any song during a worship celebration:

☐ **Before you start, determine a reasonable tempo and find a singable key.**

☐ **If the people are using books, be sure they have a means of knowing what song to sing at what time.**

☐ **Be ready to begin a song on time. (Stay awake and keep your music handy!)**

☐ **Give a clear introduction to the song so that people know exactly when to start.**

☐ **Provide a clear, easy to follow accompaniment.**

☐ **Communicate with the people during the song.**

☐ **If you make a mistake, do what is necessary to correct the error, and then proceed with confidence.**

Make it apparent by the way you lead the music that you expect the people to sing. The people are gathered to celebrate and to be personally involved and active in the celebration. You are only leading and helping their participation. From time to time, you may have to remind them gently that you are not there to provide a performance.

BEING A PERSON OF PRAYER

The minister of music is a leader of prayer. When the music minister takes the lead in certain parts of the celebration, he or she is in fact the leader of the whole celebrating community. This is a tremendous responsibility. You are calling people to pray in a very special way — through music. To lead the people in prayer, you must have a good personal prayer life, and you must be able to pray yourself during the celebration.

It is important that you are able to pray while you play and sing. This capability is important for you personally — and it is essential to conveying a prayerful spirit in your music. You may find that the tension of trying to do the music well is a total distraction from what you ordinarily consider to be praying. Be open to a fuller understanding of prayer which permits you to experience prayer while deeply involved in other activity.

Prayer can be understood in many ways, and there are many forms of prayer. A very simple description of prayer is that it is **being with God.** In his book **A Balanced Life of Prayer** Thomas Merton calls prayer, "a vital and loving awareness of the presence of God." Try to be with God as you play music and sing. This is possible even when you are distracted or are paying close attention to a difficult spot in the music. Through what you are actively doing as a minister of music, you can be brought to that vital and loving awareness of the presence of God.

Ministers of music should be people of prayer who live in daily life that which they sing about. Your daily example is important to the faith life of the people who worship with you. If people come to feel that you are not a loving, praying person, then they may not find it easy to pray with you in the liturgy. You might get them to sing with you, but it is unlikely they will be able to experience the music as prayer.

Before beginning a liturgy, or even a rehearsal, the ministers of music should pray. Praying together fifteen minutes before the start is a good practice. It is an important preparation.

I believe personally that these simple ideas on prayer are quite important for musicians who want to minister. Despite this emphasis, be assured that this does not advocate the tendency of some church musicians to believe that a lot of prayer is a substitute for planning and practice. Believe in the power of prayer — but do not rely on weekly miracles in order to do your job right!

THE NECESSITY OF PREPARATION

Good celebrations do not just fall together fifteen minutes before they begin. Preparation is indispensable. Some of this preparation takes place months in advance, while much of it takes place minutes before the liturgy begins. A responsible leader knows the necessity of being prepared. You remain a leader only as long as you are a step or two ahead of those who follow.

There are many ways to organize your preparation. The actual amount of preparation depends upon both the demands of your situation and on your personality and abilities. Some people have detailed calendars and weekly checklists, while others are able to operate with all the information in their heads. Find a way which is practical for you and those with whom you work.

LONG RANGE PLANNING

While much of life is unpredictable, the church musician is fortunate in that much of the work ahead is quite predictable, thanks to the liturgical calendar of the Church. In spite of this convenient predictability, many people get caught with nothing but alleluias to sing on the First Sunday of Lent.

As you look ahead to the liturgical seasons, consider these basic questions:

- ☐ **What new music will you have for each season of the year?**
- ☐ **When do you need to order music in order to have it on time?**
- ☐ **When do you need to begin rehearsing new music for the season?**
- ☐ **What acclamations and propers will you use for each season?**
- ☐ **When would be the best time to take your vacation?**

When you have all this information on a calendar, you can refer to it often and add information as the year progresses. Save each year's calendar to help you prepare for the next.

SHORT RANGE PLANNING

Try to start working on the details of celebrations well in advance of the season. This is especially important if you rehearse with a full choir or a small group. Published or printed materials necessary for such rehearsal must be purchased or prepared in advance. About a month before the season (Advent, Christmas, Lent, etc.), try to do the following:

- ☐ **Look at the readings and psalms for the whole season.**
- ☐ **Make some preliminary choices of music for each Sunday.**
- ☐ **Plan a rehearsal schedule.**
- ☐ **Meet with the celebrants and celebration team to plan possible themes for the upcoming Masses.**

PREPARATION DURING THE WEEK

During the week preceding the celebration(s), do the following:

☐ **Re-read the Scriptures.**

☐ **Meet with the celebrant.**

☐ **Make a detailed outline of the music planned, with several copies.**

☐ **Rehearse.**

Early in the week prepare a list of the music, meet with the celebrant and give him a copy. Check with him to make sure that the songs match the spirit of the celebration and the homily.

Regardless of whether you do the music by yourself or with a whole choir, you need to rehearse. Try not to leave anything to chance. It is a good idea to rehearse in the church itself, using the very music stands, chairs, microphones and other fixtures that you use in the celebration.

If you rehearse with a group, let the group know exactly what will be done on Sunday. By proceeding in an orderly fashion through the business at hand, you can help the group to feel prepared and at ease. It is important to explain the choices of music to them, to speak about the Scripture readings. Hopefully, such communication will improve the whole group's leadership of the congregation and enhance its performance. Finally, it is important to begin the rehearsal with prayer, to set the rehearsal in the context of the ministry you are performing.

LAST MINUTE PREPARATIONS

Immediately before the celebration begins, there are still some important things for you to do, or to make sure that **someone** is doing. You might like to develop a checklist of the weekly details.

Such a checklist may include:

☐ **Music in order?**

☐ **Numbers on the hymn board?**

☐ **Sound system OK?**

☐ **Instruments tuned?**

☐ **Do readers, other ministers understand your cues?**

☐ **Do other musicians know what leader of song will do during the Preparation Before Mass?**

Before the Mass, it is so very important to make sure that everyone (celebrant, readers, and the other musicians) understands the details. Check especially with lectors who sometimes read the Psalms or Gospel acclamations you intended to sing. If you have many things to do before the celebration, come early enough and also find someone reliable to help you.

PREPARING THE PEOPLE FOR WORSHIP

Before the Mass actually begins, it is important to practice any new music with the people. If worship is to be a life-giving experience, new songs and acclamations need to be introduced! This final bit of preparation is necessary if people are going to participate fully. It is important that you plan this brief time of preparation carefully. Keep in mind that these final minutes are not only a song practice but a preparation for the whole celebration for everyone. Good practice calls for the celebrant himself to begin this period, turning over the music details to you after a brief welcome. Irregardless of the particular practice in your parish, remember the importance of this preparation period.

Greet the people warmly. If the celebrant or leader has not already done so, briefly explain that they are asked to take this time because it is necessary — so that they can participate more fully, so that they can learn new music.

Give them an idea right away of how many things they are going to practice. This helps them settle into the ryhthm of the session. If necessary, tell them how they are to locate the various songs in their participation aid.

A recommended practice is to brush up or clean up something that they already know. Make them feel good about their improvement. Limit yourself to practicing only a few items. If too much is rehearsed, people tend to either resent it or not remember it, a bad way to begin a liturgy.

Speak loudly and clearly! It is often helpful to ask if you can be heard in the back. A "final" opportunity to adjust either the sound system

13

or your speaking level. Do not let this practice become routine. Never use more than five minutes. Be friendly and supportive, but encourage strong participation. Never be afraid to ask them to do it again if you feel they are not trying. Stay calm, however; make the preparation experience pleasant, for you are setting the mood for the entire celebration! If people in your parish complain that this preparation interferes with their desire for private prayer, the celebrant, leader, or you yourself must suggest that they should come a little earlier.

A cardinal rule: do not waste time. As soon as people are doing a decent job on a song, whether old or new, STOP them in a friendly and complimentary way and move on. The rehearsal is indispensable, but it should never last more than five minutes.

WHAT WENT WRONG?

No matter how adequately you thought you had prepared, something probably will go wrong. A million humorous stories could be told on this point. However, to show that mistakes are timeless and probably inescable, we share a story from Saint Augustine, Fourth Century (from **Exposition on the Psalms**, preface to Psalm 138):

> We had prepared us a short psalm and desired the reader to chant it, but he, through confusion at the time as it seems, has substituted another for it. We have chosen the will of God in the reader's mistake, rather than our own, so we will proceed with his purpose.

A celebration will never happen just as it was planned. That may be the doing of a forgetful lector, or of the Holy Spirit. And, if you are the one who made the mistake — learn from it, if there is anything really to learn, and then don't lose sleep over it!

II.
Music in
Eucharistic Worship

OVERVIEW

As a minister of music to Catholic communities, you usually will be playing/leading/singing music for a Eucharistic liturgy. To understand how music can best be used at Mass, we should look at the structure of the liturgy. We will then consider the parts where music is of foremost importance. Afterwards, we can look at all other places in the Mass where music is possible.

Often, Catholic musicians simply are not familiar with the dynamics and structure of the Mass in its present form. Few parishes were really instructed about the changes that took place in the Mass after the Second Vatican Council. We knew the Mass was in English, and that some new parts were added such as the sign of peace. We saw that the prayers at the foot of the altar were dropped, as was the last Gospel. We suddenly learned that the prayers after Mass were not part of the Mass. I urge you to read other books or even pamphlets for explanations of why the Mass was changed, if you have not had the opportunity to learn. Here, we must concentrate on the form and structure of the Mass as it presently is celebrated, so that you can understand how to provide appropriate music.

There are two major parts of the Mass:
The Liturgy of the Word, and
The Liturgy of the Eucharist.
Both liturgies are important to a complete experiencing of Christ in the Mass. Our God is not silent, nor distant. He is present in His Word and in His Body. We celebrate the events of human salvation as we hear them told in the Liturgy of the Word, and then we are invited to participate in the saving sacrifice of Christ during the Liturgy of the Eucharist.

Places
and
Priorities
for
Music
in
Eucharistic
Worship

"These two acts are so closely connected as to form one act of worship. The table of the Lord is the table of God's Word and Christ's Body, and from it the faithful are instructed and refreshed."
(General Instruction on the Roman Missal, No. 7).

In addition to these two liturgies, there are short rites of entrance, preparation and dismissal. These ritualize the gathering and scattering of the People of God, and they are considered secondary in importance.

THE ACCLAMATIONS

Both the Liturgy of the Word and the Liturgy of the Eucharist have identifiable high points. Corresponding to these high points are times for song that we call "acclamations." These are comparatively brief songs. Unfortunately, these acclamations are merely spoken without much attention in many parishes — yet, these acclamations are the most important times for singing in the entire Mass. They are parts of the Mass which **always** should be sung. Singing the acclamations lets the whole community express itself at the high points of the celebration.

In the Liturgy of the Word, the central event is the proclamation of the Gospel, for Christ Himself is present and speaking to us as His words of Good News are proclaimed. To greet the proclamation of the Gospel, we sing an alleluia verse. This acclamation of joy prepares us to hear the Gospel, as we all stand together.

The central event of the Liturgy of the Eucharist is the Eucharistic Prayer. The Words of Institution are the high point, though not independent from the whole Prayer. The Eucharistic Prayer is the main prayer of the Church. The Eucharistic Prayer is begun by everyone present by a sung acclamation, the "Holy Holy." It is concluded by yet another acclamation, the singing of the Great Amen. By this song, we all affirm that this is indeed our Prayer.

The central event of the Eucharistic Prayer, the Words of Institution, calls for response in song. In singing the Memorial Acclamation, in its many possible variations, we affirm our principal beliefs about Jesus — that He died for our sins, that He rose from death, and that He will come again.

Even if it is not possible to have much singing at a given Mass, it is these acclamations which really should be sung, if nothing else. Singing highlights and intensifies our worship experience. Therefore, it stands to reason that the high points of that experience deserve first consideration in planning music for the Mass. This understanding of the primary importance of sung acclamations is based on the statements of the Bishops' Committee on the Liturgy as well as the pastoral opinions of almost all liturgical authors.

Unfortunately, many church musicians are surprisingly unfamiliar with the basic structure of the Mass and its primary calls for song. Rather than singing the acclamations, many of them typically provide a processional, "offertory song", communion song and recessional. Some call this the "four hymn syndrome." Others call it "liturgical travelling music", since this pattern provides music only when the celebrant travels in or out, when the collection is taken and when people walk to communion. This pattern has its origins in the Latin Mass, which could accomodate songs in English (or other native languages) only at certain points. To state the situation as bluntly as possible, this approach to music programming is totally outdated.

To be an effective minister of music for today's Church, it is essential that you find (or write!) good acclamations, that you play and lead them and teach them well to the people, and that you "program" them effectively in accord with the ebb and flow of the celebration. The acclamations come at the important moments of celebration. If you only work with the four hymns, you are only a "minister of transportation." Sorry!

THE EUCHARISTIC CELEBRATION AND THE USE OF MUSIC WITHIN IT

The Entrance Rite

The entrance rite consists of:
    Opening song
    Greeting
    Penitential Rite
    Glory to God
    Prayer

The entrance rite celebrates our gathering. It should prepare us as in-

Places
and
Priorities
for
Music
in
Eucharistic
Worship

17

dividuals and as a community to celebrate. It should be short so as not to overshadow or delay the more important Liturgy of the Word.

OPENING SONG: The celebration should begin with an opening song. This song is definitely part of this rite. Don't end the song on cue when the celebrant reaches the altar — finish it! This song celebrates our unity and our gathering. It may also reflect the theme and spirit of the day's celebration. After the acclamations, this is one of the most important times to sing.

PENITENTIAL RITE: There are several options for the form of the penitential rite, and some of them may be used with music. As a rule, this rite is not sung unless you want to emphasize the penitential motif, as is appropriate during Lent. If the optional rite of sprinkling is used, provide some music during the action. A congregational hymn of baptism or cleansing is appropriate. A solo or instrumental piece also would work well.

GLORY TO GOD: This is a Hymn of Praise. It is meant to be sung; otherwise it should not be used at all. The Gloria is used only on Sundays and feasts outside Lent and Advent. It may be sung by everyone, or only by the choir or music group. Most available arrangements which call for everyone to sing everything are tedious. Look for arrangements which give the people repeated antiphonal sections to sing, leaving the rest to you or your group.

*   *   *

THE LITURGY OF THE WORD

The Liturgy of the Word consists of these parts:

The First Reading, from the Old Testament
The Response (Responsorial Psalm)
The Second Reading, from the New Testament

The Gospel Acclamation (Alleluia)
The Gospel Reading
The Homily

The Creed, when appropriate
The Prayer of the Faithful

The Word of God is proclaimed to the community during the Liturgy of the Word. We are nourished through the readings which reveal God's love and redemption of us. We listen to the Word, digest it with the aid of silence and the Homily, and respond to it through Psalms and the Creed.

RESPONSORIAL PSALM

A period of silence separates the Old Testament reading from the singing of the Responsorial Psalm. Since the Psalms were written as songs, they ought to be sung. It is recommended that the entire community sing the antiphon, while a cantor (soloist) sings the verses. Other formats include:

- ☐ singing the antiphon and speaking the verses
- ☐ singing the psalm all the way through
- ☐ substituting a song containing the psalm text
- ☐ instrumental music, with the psalm read as a meditation.

All of these options are preferred to just reading the psalm. Singing the Responsorial Psalm not only gives the people a chance to respond to the Word of God, but also serves to vary the action of the liturgy. If everything is verbal, people's attention slips away. St. Ambrose of Milan noticed this in the Fourth Century! He wrote:

> "The success of this experiment (singing antiphonal psalms) was very great, for the congregation, which nothing could induce to keep quiet during the readings immediately stopped making any further disturbance once the psalms started and joined in singing with enthusiasm."
> (F. Van Der Meer, **Augustine the Bishop**, Harper & Row, 336).

People today might have good reason to be just as bored with the liturgy, unfortunately, but at least they are more polite during the readings!

GOSPEL ACCLAMATION

The Gospel Acclamation introduces the Gospel and is not a response to the previous reading. A period of silence follows the Second Reading, after which the leader of song asks everyone to rise and sing the Gospel Acclamation. After the reading of the Gospel, you can sing the refrain again. On occasion, it is also effective to repeat this antiphon again after

Places
and
Priorities
for
Music
in
Eucharistic
Worship

the homily, especially if the homily has been brief and directly related to the Gospel, as it should be.

The acclamation should be joyous and easy to sing. It consists of an antiphon, sung by all the people, a verse sung by a cantor or choir, and a repetition of the antiphon. The antiphon usually is a series of sung alleluias. During Lent, alternative texts are used. The verse between the antiphons may be the one that is provided for the day, or you may choose one for the whole season. If you sing a version of the Gospel acclamation that has several verses, **choose only the most suitable one.** If several verses are sung, the acclamation becomes a song and ceases to be an acclamation.

PROFESSION OF FAITH (CREED)

In most cases, the Creed should not be sung. The Creed should be professed by **everyone,** and there are very few settings or versions of the Creed which allow everyone to sing comfortably, mainly because it is quite long. From time to time, a sung version with an antiphon repeated by the people can be used.

PRAYERS OF THE FAITHFUL (INTERCESSIONS)

If the occasion is very festive or solemn, the responses of the people to the prayers of the Faithful may be sung. The cantor should lead everyone in these responses. They should be simple and brief. Musically, this is a low priority, and singing at this time is not recommended as a normal practice.

Because it is possible to repeat the Gospel acclamation several times, and because it is possible to sing the Creed, to sing the Prayers of the Faithful, and also to have a song during the Preparation of the Gifts immediately following the Liturgy of the Word, you must be careful not to overload this anticlimatic time of the celebration with singing.

Preparation of the Gifts

The Liturgy of the Eucharist has an introductory rite called the Preparation of the Gifts. It is definitely "secondary", just like the entrance rite and the conclusion. Therefore, it should not be dragged out, nor should it overshadow the Liturgy it introduces. The Preparation of the Gifts consists of these parts:

> Procession of Gifts to the Altar
> Preparation of Gifts on the Altar
> Prayer Over the Gifts

This rite is a good time for instrumental music, solos or choral pieces. The people deserve a breather between the two major parts of the celebration. If there is singing from time to time, it should not add to the length of the rite. There are varying opinions about whether any music at this time should cover the brief prayers of the priest preparing the bread and wine. It is not a crucial issue. Also, you should be aware that liturgists consider it important that the actions and singing during the Preparation of the Gifts do not become confusing signs by emphasizing the notion of "offering" or "offertory." The true offering takes place during the Eucharistic Prayer.

[**Editor's Note:** Various authorities go to some length in explaining that this rite is not like the old Offertory of the Latin Mass. The result is that much is written about what the preparation of the gifts is **not.** However, the bringing of the gifts and the gestures of the celebrant with them during the preparation still communicate the idea of "offering" quite plainly. Therefore, we feel it is better to concentrate upon the general principle that this rite should be brief, simple and secondary, rather than to elaborate upon what it supposedly is not. Since much of the confusion lies in the signs, actions and history of this rite, the main task of the music minister is to use appropriate music and perhaps to stay away from songs which plainly emphasize the offering of bread and wine.]

*   *   *

Places
and
Priorities
for
Music
in
Eucharistic
Worship

THE LITURGY OF THE EUCHARIST

*** The Liturgy of the Eucharist is celebrated in two parts, the Eucharistic Prayer, and the Communion Rite. Together they constitute the single Eucharist and should not be thought of as separate or independent from each other.

THE EUCHARISTIC PRAYER

The Eucharistic Prayer consists of these parts:

Preface
- **First Acclamation (Holy Holy)**
  Invocation of the Holy Spirit ("Epiclesis")
  Words of Institution
- **Second Acclamation (Memorial)**
  Memorial Prayer ("Anamnesis")
  Intercessions
- **Third Acclamation (Doxology and Amen)**

The Eucharistic Prayer of thanksgiving and sanctification is the central event of the celebration. The three acclamations provide everyone with important opportunities to respond to the Prayer proclaimed by the priest. The acclamations also help to keep the Eucharistic Prayer from being an excessively "verbal" experience.

HOLY HOLY (First Acclamation)

This acclamation is sung by everyone at the end of the Preface to the Eucharistic Prayer. In it we join with all the angels and saints in acclaiming the Lord. The Holy Holy should always be sung by everyone, never just by a choir or music group.

There are many versions of this acclamation. Every celebrating community should have several that they know very well and can sing without books. If you introduce a new version, it should be the main focus of the rehearsal before Mass, so that it may be sung strongly and with ease by all. It is very important that the Holy Holy be an immediate and vigorous response to the celebrant's climatic conclusion of the Preface, "...**we join the angels and saints in proclaiming your glory as we sing . . .**" This is a critical time for the music people to have their act really together. There must be no delay or unnecessary instrumental introduction between the celebrant's last word and the first "Holy." The people themselves should understand the desire for a strong response at this time. If they need music, they should know where to find it without announcements. One way to have a smooth beginning of the singing is for the instrumental introduction to begin during the words of the Preface, providing an ever-building background for the proclamation of the celebrant. These principles apply to all the acclamations.

MEMORIAL (Second Acclamation)

A response to the invitation, "Let Us Proclaim the Mystery of Our Faith!", this acclamation is our statement of faith in the paschal mystery that is occurring. In it we proclaim our principal beliefs about Christ: that He died for our sins, rose again in glory, and will come again.

There are four suggested texts for this acclamation, and you should vary their use. Choose music settings that are truly singable and which have the "feel" of an acclamation. Also, be aware that a number of very beautiful acclamations have been written with original texts differing from the familiar ones. The use of these alternative texts is quite acceptable.

Remember: avoid delays in singing caused by not being prepared or by unreasonably long introductions.

GREAT AMEN (Third Eucharistic Acclamation)

This Amen is the affirmation and assent of everyone present to the Eucharistic Prayer. The group should know by heart several strong sung versions. Consider versions which are musically related to other acclamations in the same Mass; this helps reinforce the continuity of the whole Eucharistic Prayer. Also, many Amen settings have companion melodies for the preceding doxology. The doxology is sung by the whole group in some places, depending on local interpretation of the liturgical norms. A sung doxology, whether with everyone or solely by the celebrant, provides a smooth musical introduction for the Amen itself, eliminating the chance for delay. Remember, too, that the Amen can be done quite powerfully with no instruments other than everyone's voices.

Places
and
Priorities
for
Music
in
Eucharistic
Worship

COMMUNION RITE

The Communion Rite consists of these parts:

The Lord's Prayer
Sign of Peace
Breaking of the Bread
Lamb of God
Communion
Prayer After Communion

"The necessary and inevitable conclusion of the Eucharistic Prayer is the Communion of Jesus with his Father, of the Father with Jesus, of Jesus with us, of us with Jesus, of us with the Father, of us with one another."

—Fr. Eugene A. Walsh, S.S.

During the rite of Communion, we enter into a relationship with the Father through Christ as we pray the Lord's Prayer. We recognize that Christ is present in our neighbor as well as in ourselves during the Sign of Peace. The perfect sign of our communion is in the eating and drinking as He instructed us to do.

There are many opportunities for singing and music during the rite of Communion. It is the responsibility of the music minister, in cooperation with the whole celebrating team, to plan just the right times and amounts of music for each celebration, so that it is effective and not overdone.

THE LORD'S PRAYER

This is the most universally known prayer there is — yet we can easily prevent participation in this prayer if we use difficult, unfamiliar or bad music. The Lord's Prayer may be sung, if you have carefully learned a good musical version in which everyone can join. To leave room for other variety in the Communion Rite, it is strongly recommended that the Lord's Prayer not be sung as a matter of regular routine. There are **some** good musical settings for this prayer, but not many. Be selective. Remember that it is better for this prayer to be spoken well (quite a challenge in itself), than to use poor music, or to sing it too often.

DOXOLOGY TO THE LORD'S PRAYER

At the end of the Our Father, the celebrant continues with a brief prayer, and then everyone responds, "For the kingdom, the power, and the glory are yours, now and forever." This doxology may be sung, even if you choose not to sing the entire prayer. As with other responses and acclamations, this response should be familiar and sung spontaneously.

SIGN OF PEACE

During the Sign of Peace you may choose to sing an appropriate song. It is best if this is done by only the musicians so as not to limit the people's participation in the Gesture of Peace. This song should be short and should not significantly lengthen the rite.

LAMB OF GOD

The "Lamb of God" is a litany to accompany the breaking of the bread, in preparation for communion. This litany has an invocation (Lamb of God who takes away the sins of the world) and a response (Have mercy on us). It may be repeated as often as the action demands (i.e., if there is a real breaking of the bread that takes some time), with the final response always being "Grant us peace." You may sing it in the alternating litany form or as a continuous song. The invocation may be sung by just the choir, with everyone singing the response.

THE COMMUNION SONG

A primary consideration about songs during the reception of Communion is that they not demand undue effort from the people receiving communion. The minister of music has a wide range of options for very effective communion music.

It is not necessary that the people sing constantly during communion. If they sing on their way to communion, choose a song with a short, easily-memorized chorus, leaving the verses to a soloist or choir. The people should not have to carry books or papers with them, especially now that they have the option of receiving communion in the hand.

**Places
and
Priorities
for
Music
in
Eucharistic
Worship**

If the time for communion is long enough for several musical pieces, use some variety, including some silence. This is a good time to use choirs, soloist, or instrumental music. You may choose to have one song in the beginning that is sung by everybody, with the rest of the music handled by the choir or musicians.

The music chosen for communion should be capable of uniting the congregation, helping them experience together the joy of unity in the Body of Christ. In making your choices, also consider the spirit and nature of the particular celebration. There are no fixed rules for communion music. Use your creativity and judgement well.

COMMUNION MEDITATION MUSIC

After communion there is a period of silent prayer and meditation. Sometimes music can enhance this period. Music should be done only if it helps people pray. If there was a lot of communion music, perhaps silence is the best song. However, sometimes it is hard to experience silence in large groups or distracting places. Some instrumental music can help.

SONG OF THANKSGIVING

After the silent prayer, you might sing a Song of Thanksgiving. If you did not have congregational singing during the distribution of communion, this is a good time to have a song that expresses oneness and thanksgiving. In many places, this is the final song of the celebration.

Between the Great Amen and a possible "closing song" we have seen seven times in the communion rite for possible singing. You must be careful not to plan too much singing during this period. Vary your format from Sunday to Sunday. Choose music and times for singing that genuinely enhance the flow of the celebration. It is better to have too little music than too much.

Dismissal Rite

The Dismissal Rite consists of a Blessing and the Dismissal.

THE RECESSIONAL SONG(?)

The "Recessional Song" has never been an official part of the rite. There is an immediate contradiction if the final words of the liturgy are "The Mass is ended, go in peace" and the musician says, in effect, "No, wait, and we will sing Hymn 24." Usually the people want to obey the priest, so they start putting on their coats and banging the kneelers. A few people half-heartedly join in the singing, but a few more use it as an opportunity to beat the crowds to the parking lot. This is not a very satisfying conclusion for our worship. Do a recessional piece with only the choir, or use a brisk instrumental postlude. If you are bound by some tradition that obligates you to sing a recessional song, choose something short and lively.

*　　*　　*

SUMMARY

When planning the music for Mass, the most important places for everyone to sing are the **Acclamations**. These should be sung even at masses where little else is sung. They are:

The Gospel Acclamation
The Holy, Holy, Holy
The Memorial Acclamation
The Great Amen

The next priority is to try to provide music for the following:

Entrance/Opening Song
Responsorial Psalm
Communion and/or Thanksgiving Song

Beyond these, it is a matter of individual choice, based on the needs and best interests of the people and the celebration. Any additional singing is supplementary.

Places
and
Priorities
for
Music
in
Eucharistic
Worship

III.
Choosing Music
for Celebration

STYLE OF MUSIC

There are many styles of music. No one style can be called "sacred"; no one style can be labeled profane or unworthy of use in a church. A melody, or style of playing a melody is a neutral element. How we **interpret** music is what gives it value for us.

Gregorian chant is acknowledged as "proper to the Roman liturgy," but this is not because the melody is sacred. It is because we have a rich tradition of sacred music written in that style. For many people the melodies themselves may connote the sacred because of long exposure to that tradition. But chant melodies can also be found in rather unsacred cults, not to mention rather irreverent lyrics created by seminarians over the years.

Many of our oldest and finest hymns have taken the tunes of popular songs of their day. St. Ambrose of Milan, Martin Luther and Charles Wesley all borrowed melodies from songs already popular in the secular culture, putting "sacred" lyrics to them.

One of the best examples of a tune that has gone through this process is the song we now know as "O Sacred Head, Now Wounded." Our hymnals avoid mentioning its origin by simply crediting the melody to Hans Leo Hassler. The fact is that the melody is found in a collection of popular German songs edited by Hassler in 1601. It was originally a love song about a man who thinks his girl does not love him any more. It probably would be a country western hit today. Do these secular origins make the melody any less sacred today? No! Nor does the song, "An American Tune", written by

Paul Simon (of Simon and Garfunkel) in 1972 become sacred, even though he uses the same tune.

Martin Luther defended the practice of using commonly known folk tunes for religious music. He felt it was not necessary for ". . . the devil to usurp all the beautiful melodies." Many Catholics may not want to use Martin Luther as the last word for justifying the use of popular music for our worship, but this reminder of where our "sacred" melodies come from helps to establish that it is not the tune that makes the hymn sacred.

Hymns are not made sacred by the types of instruments used for accompaniment. People may well find it easier to pray with certain instruments, but this is a matter of association and culture. For centuries the Christian Church in the West allowed no instruments in the churches. Until the ninth century, the organ connoted bawdy pagan orgies to the people. So, in that culture, the organ did not help people to pray.

Presently, in our culture, the organ remains the most widely accepted instrument for leading people in prayer. The Constitution on the Liturgy affirms that:
> "In the Latin Church, the pipe organ is to be held in high esteem, for it is the traditional musical instrument and one that adds a wonderful splendor to the Church's ceremonies and powerfully lifts up the mind to God and heavenly things." (No. 120).

The same document goes on to say that other instruments may also be admitted for use in worship. In our culture, there are many instruments that can be used for the praise and worship of God, if they are played competently. Psalm 150 says that all kinds of instruments were used to praise God in the temple. The psalm mentions stringed instruments, trumpets, drums, reed and wind instruments, and cymbals. Any instrument is appropriate in worship if it helps people pray and celebrate.

Good pastoral judgement by the minister of music is necessary in choosing the style of music that will bring people closer to God in worship. Sometimes this judgement is difficult in a pluralistic culture such as we have in this country. Musical taste varies with ethnic background, age, sophistication and personal differences. Within this country, there are many kinds of music that are valid expressions of our people's culture and musical taste — here is a partial list of the styles of music we see being used in our churches today:

Gregorian chant
Other chant forms
Hymns from a variety of past periods in history
Modern hymns in a traditional style
Modern hymns of an experimental nature
Folk music — both traditional and modern
Contemporary music with guitar accompaniment
Gospel music — traditional and popular
Latin American music
Rock and pop music
African music
Country, western music
Polka music
Bluegrass music
Native American music
Jazz music

These are all distinctive styles of music and there are many categories in between. They all have their place in our worship. All of them are legitimate expressions of the musical heritage and culture of American Catholics. Good jugement will tell you if a musical style is suitable for a particular community. You should not employ different kinds of music as a novelty or gimmick. A polka Mass may be a meaningful expression of faith in parts of Wisconsin or Minnesota. The music is part of the soul of the people. The same music might be totally out of place in other communities.

The question arises of how to deal with parishes with mixed preferences and backgrounds. First, there must be a recognition of this mixture. Then, we must remember that most people in this country, even if they do not have a European background, were brought up with religious music from the European tradition. For most parishes, therefore, this music should be the core for a majority of the celebrations. Most parishes have several masses: one of them can easily offer an alternative style of music. In a large parish, you can offer several options.

The wrong style of music can destroy people's ability to pray, so try to offer alternative choices. We will never be able to make everyone happy all the time. That is the nature of living in a community.

"Each Christian must keep in mind that to live and worship in community often demands a personal sacrifice. Everyone must be willing to share likes and dislikes with those whose ideas and experiences may be quite unlike their own."
(Music in Catholic Worship, No. 17.)

QUALITY OF THE MUSIC

If music is to help people pray, it must be of sufficient quality to make prayer possible. Poor music cannot accomplish this. At worst, it can make prayer impossible. What makes a piece of music "good"? It is hard to agree on a set of technical details that make a melody good. For the most part, to be honest, judgements of "quality" are quite subjective. There are, however, generally accepted characteristics in a quality melody. We should consider three of them.

A good song should:
☐   be easy to sing
☐   be easy to remember
☐   endure over time.

Singability is a characteristic of a good tune. A good song will not tax a congregation's ability by jumping spasmodically from one unpredictable tone to another. It also is easier if a song has a comfortable range of pitch. The "Star Spangled Banner" is not easy to sing, even if you are standing, because it has such a wide range. If a song is singable, it will be **enjoyed** by the whole group, not just endured. Hymns and songs are not meant to be suffered through as a form of penance.

It is hard to put a finger on what makes a tune **memorable**, but most good songs and hymns are easily memorized. The Halleluiah Chorus, Beethoven's Ninth Symphony, and many pieces of Gregorian Chant have this characteristic. Good music sticks in our minds. Memorability does not in itself make a good tune, but it is definitely characteristic of good music. Memorable songs are easily learned by a congregation and become a part of its life outside worship. St. Augustine once mentioned that he often observed the people singing the Psalms during the week as they worked — because they liked the melodies! A memoriable tune blended with good words will become an expression of prayer for people outside of liturgy as well.

Choosing
and
Evaluating
Music
for
Worship

31

There are many songs that are both singable and memorable, yet they will not **endure** for very long. For example, a jingle for a cola or a hamburger franchise is catchy, but it does not take too long for you to say, "If I hear that song one more time . . . .(!!!) . . ." A song of quality has durability. This cannot be determined right after a song has been written, but experience will help you identify the trite melody and the musical cliche. Music that endures often becomes a source of strength and reassurance for people in crisis. For example, when the Titanic sank, the band played a familiar hymn to comfort the passengers. People in danger or pain often choose to sing a familiar religious song. In times when prayer is difficult, a song is often easier.

These characteristics of quality music should help you recognize pieces that are suitable for worship. Seek out the opinions of experienced musicians to help you, remembering that judgements of "triteness" and so forth can often be very subjective. There really is no objective measure of quality — ultimately, you do need to trust your own judgement and experience.

CONSIDER THE ORIGINAL CONTEXT

There are many cases in which music from "secular" sources is most effective as music for worship, especially instrumental music. Since we have, in fact, argued that no tune should be written off as "secular" or canonized as "sacred", a note of common sense is in order. If you do use song from pop, film, or other non-liturgical sources, **consider their original context** in judging their suitability for use in worship. An instrumental rendition of a song of rather passionate romance may distract people who are familiar with the original words. The music of "Tubular Bells" by Mike Oldfield may make an impressive and festive organ piece, but its association with the movie **The Exorcist** gives it a connotation of evil, making it most questionable as liturgical music. Use careful judgement!

TEXTS

"A song is hardly worth singing (in church) — even if we like the tune — unless it has a text that really says something."

(**Liturgy Committee Handbook**, Virginia Sloyan, ed., The Liturgical Conference, p. 86.).

A minister of music needs to sort through the thousands of hymns and songs that have been written, choosing those which really are appropriate for contemporary worship. Equal attention must be given to the texts as is given to the music. Good texts should flow like poetry (not necessarily rhyme and meter) and be consistent with contemporary use of the language. As a matter of fact **poetry** is precisely what we do look for in such texts. Good poetry captures a worthwhile thought in a few well-chosen words, in a way that stirs our imagination and clings to our memory. These texts should be liturgically appropriate, theologically sound, and have a root, however subtle, in Scripture.

We have many songs which were composed for Christians in another age. We no longer live, think or speak as they did. Most hymnals published before 1970 are overloaded with these songs. The use of words like "lo" or "vouchsafe" or "beseech" conveys a stilted image of our faith and only reinforces the unfortunate opinion that the liturgy is irrelevant to contemporary life. In addition, avoid hymns which contain saccharine language or metaphors that are gruesome or outdated. We no longer live in a rural agricultural society, sail our ships or fight battles wearing armor. The songs we sing should reflect the experience of the Gospel for twentieth-century Christians. Note, however, that many of the best hymns do have a universality that speaks to our experience today as well as they did when they were written. These hymns should be sought out and used.

On the other hand, not every song that mentions love, joy, peace, slums, minorities, pollution and ballistic missiles is necessarily appropriate for contemporary celebration. Many new songs have trite, didactic, dated or theologically unsound texts. Others have sing-song lyrics of poor quality that do not reflect or increase people's faith. Such songs should not be used in worship.

SEXIST LANGUAGE IN MUSIC FOR WORSHIP

The English language does have some weaknesses in dealing with gender that are not the fault of us today. Women are well aware of this

Choosing
and
Evaluating
Music
for
Worship

33

difficulty and usually are not unreasonable about it. However, the fact remains that music should **unite** people at worship. If we continue to use song texts which blatantly exclude the majority of the community, we simply are not serving that community. There are hundreds of songs in frequent use today that simply do not sufficiently reflect the fact that women are also members of the Body of Christ. Consider a few examples:

Good Christian Men, Rejoice!

Once to Every Man and Nation

O Brother Man

Lord Christ, When Thou first came to Men

Faith of Our Fathers

"Contemporary" songs are no better in this regard, contributing titles like:

Sons of God

Brothers in Christ

Man of Mind

Whatsoever You Do to the Least of My Brothers

I Am My Brother's Brother

Do whatever you can to eliminate songs or verses with language that is obviously offensive to the women of our Church. Any song which refers to Christians as "men" or "brothers" should be used for worship only if the celebrating community happens to be all male. There might be varying opinions on how well the terms such as "man" refer to all people, but the fact remains that many women do not feel that such words really include them. There are many things, quite uncontrollable by most of us, in our Church which divide us. However, our worship should unite us. Certainly, we should not allow language to separate and alienate us. It is not difficult to find songs that are not sexist, or to avoid using verses with that sort of language.

A separate issue can be that of the "gender" of God in our music. We know that Christ was male and therefore is referred to as "he", etc. How to refer to the One God, Yahweh, is more problematic. Some do not like the name "Yahweh" on the grounds that it violates Jewish sensitivities about referring to God. Others are sensitive to terms which limit God by sex or gender. The responsibility of music ministers is to be aware of the sensitivities of the community which they serve, and to use music which will give a full experience of God and unify a divided people in celebration.

IV.
Some
Practical
Matters

THE WORTH OF A MUSIC MINISTER — IN DOLLARS

It requires skill to be an effective musician, plus years of experience to refine that skill and to develop a suitable repertoire. It also takes constant work to discover the best new material available. It also takes time to prepare sufficiently for each Sunday, time to choose music, time to meet with the celebrant, and time to practice. These are regular and **professional** demands made upon ministers of music. Given the realities of this world's life, they deserve payment. Even if these tasks are not the sole occupation of the parish musician, people who have major and regular responsibility for music at liturgy should be considered professionals and paid accordingly.

Every parish should have a policy on who gets paid, and why, or why not. When a discussion involves money, many people start getting uncomfortable and the conversation becomes less rational. Money must be discussed, however. Salaries for professional musicians are necessary if we ever want to improve the quality of music in the Catholic Church. To clarify, let's look at the probably consequences of paying or not paying musicians.

ADVANTAGES TO THE PARISH

First, consider the advantages to the parish of NOT paying musicians. There is only one advantage, but it is definitely significant. It's **cheaper.** Money is tight in most parishes, making it impossible to pay musicians without shifting the money from other needs or programs. Such a shift would require redefining parish priorities.

Now consider the disadvantages to the parish of not paying its key music people. The parish is in a very vulnerable position if such people are not under some sort of contract or working agreement. You have no choice but to regard the minister of music as someone doing a weekly favor for the parish. If the musician refuses to plan with the celebrant or the team, there is no solution to the problem short of a major confrontation. If the musician plays poorly or chooses inappropriate music, it is difficult to demand better music. In a professional relationship, the musician expects directions and criticism. In the absence of this professional relationship, the parish is forced to consider anything it gets as better than nothing.

In additions to the disadvantages already mentioned, the parish has no control over the attendance of musicians who are on volunteer status. As a matter of fact, most musicians are more reliable than any parish has the right to expect. However, if a volunteer wishes to visit family out-of-state on Easter (the biggest Feast of the year, and also part of a holiday weekend), there is nothing you can do. You can only say, "Thank You for playing during all of Lent. Happy Easter!"

Parishes coasting with an unpaid choir director are especially foolish. Without considering the parish at large, twenty to sixty people, choir members, are relying upon a person over whom there is no control. We can be glad that many parishes have luckily filled this position with good people, but this is really no way to do it.

Beyond these obvious disadvantages, consider two important reasons why the parish should pay the musicians who have the major responsibility for music in your parish:

> 1. Worship is too important to the faith life of the people of your parish to rely on the goodwill of the best free musician you can get.

> 2. It is unfair to make continous professional demands of musicians in your parish who are not compensated as professionals.

It is hard to find a parish which has a really good music program, and this fact is reflected in the worship that is normative in most areas. Poor music in Catholic parishes should come as no surprise, since many parishes spend no more money on music than is involved in the routine monthly cost of a missalette, containing a few miscellaneous songs. These same parishes do not pay any leader of music, being content with the best leadership available for free. The old adage, "you get what you pay for" is usually true.

Consider seriously the issue of fairness and justice to people providing a significant amount of time and services to the parish. We do not ask our plumbers, lawyers or accountants to donate 5 to 20 hours weekly of their professional services to the parish. Each parish should consider seriously the needs and efforts of all its ministers and employees, and come to terms with how to treat all with fairness. What is "just" cannot be defined here; it depends on the people and place involved.

ADVANTAGES TO THE MINISTER OF MUSIC

Ministers of music probably can see obvious advantages in being paid for the work devoted to their ministry. However, when you become a paid professional, there are two areas in which you may experience changes:

a) Your relationship with the people with whom you work; and, b) these people's expectation of you.

How you are treated by people does not depend solely upon your professional/paid status. However, you should be aware that things might change when you transition from volunteer to paid status.

The change can be for better, or for worse:

- If you are a volunteer, UNPAID, your working situation can range from quite bad to quite good. You may be treated as free labor, with little appreciation shown for what you offer and do. Or, you may be highly respected and appreciated as a volunteer minister of music. Or, your situation may be somewhere in between, capable of changing to better, or to worse.

- If you become a PAID musician, the attitudes in the parish can go several ways. If you were respected as a volunteer minister of music, this respect may continue and even increase with the coming of your firmer, more professional status. If you had been treated as "free labor", your new status might bring new respect. However, it is also possible that the good relationships you enjoyed as a volunteer may degenerate into you being treated as "hired help" rather than a minister of the parish.

Good ministers of music, whether paid or volunteer, are responsible people. However you must realize that people definitely will expect more of you if you are paid. When you are not paid, it is possible to take off occasionally and not be concerned about finding a replacement. You don't to go to all the meetings that may be scheduled if you really don't want to do so. You are in the position of viewing your work as a gift donated to the parish, and that in itself is satisfying. For these reasons and others, you may not wish to be paid for your work.

If you are paid, the parish has the right to expect certain things from you. Many of these expectations are no different from what a responsible music minister would want to do anyway, even if not paid. However, it is important to identify these expectations in a written agreement, both to avoid misunderstandings and to protect yourself from inflating job expectations — both of which can be inevitable.

CONTRACTS AND WRITTEN AGREEMENTS

The parish should be specific about what the minister of music is expected to do. All expectations should be in writing, even if it is not a formal contract. Writing an agreement, a letter of intent, or simply a job description will help you talk out any problems in advance, in addition to providing something concrete for future reference.

Once you have made the agreement, **stick to it.** If something needs to be changed, change what is in writing. If the parish wants the minister of music to start doing more than was agreed, point out that these requests are beyond the existing agreement. If you cannot undertake the extra work, say so. If you want to amend the agreement, do so. If you're willing to do some of the extra work on a volunteer basis, make sure this fact is plainly understood. If music ministers do not make such matters clear, they easily become victims of inflating job expectations. The first request may simply be that of providing music for a parish picnic. But if you are not careful, it can happen that you will be **expected** to play for bingo games, meetings, private parties.

HOW MUCH TO PAY?

Setting the exact pay level for the musician is difficult. Some dioceses have guidelines. These guidelines vary greatly. Organizations such as the American Guild of Organists have published guidelines. It is not practical to give specific figures here, but pay scales should be comparable to those of similar professions, such as tutoring music or other teaching. The salary should reflect the time required and the responsibility of the minister of music. Also, the pay should reflect the individual's training and experience. If the job happens to be full-time, as is becoming the case for those with the primary music leadership roles, then salaries are easier to establish, since it goes without saying that such music ministers are entitled to a salary that realistically reflects today's cost of living.

Individual pastoral musicians vary so much that it can be difficult to set objective standards. For instance, a person with a degree in music without church experience may not be as good a minister of music as a guitarist with many years of experience in church music. Judgement and a sense of fairness is necessary in coming to these salary decisions.

In addition to the basics of salary and specific responsibilities, there are a few other things which should be contained in the agreement. First, make sure that there is one person to whom the minister of music is responsible. This could be a pastor, a parish worship coordinator, or the music director. This is essential to good communication and ongoing evaluation. Secondly, time off should be specified. If there is to be a paid vacation, the agreement should specify who is to find and pay for a substitute.

A final word. No amount of money, nor volumes of written agreements can replace a loving, Christian relationship among people. Nor is a contract any substitute for the effort and energy that must constantly be given by everyone involved to maintain a good working relationship.

KNOWING YOUR PLACE — IN THE BUILDING

As a minister of music, you should know your place in the church, the church building itself. The ministers of music do not belong in a balcony in the rear of the building. When the priest stopped facing the wall, turned around and came forward, musicians should have come out of the choir loft.

Some Practical Matters

It is not possible to effectively lead a group of people with their backs turned toward you. Architecture should not dictate practice — the choir loft can be used for seating overflow crowds. Your place in the church makes a statement about your ministry and your leadership. Even if the organ is located in the choir loft, a situation which a good organist can work with sufficiently, the rest of the music ministers belong in front. The people need visible leaders of music. Even if acoustical considerations make it preferable to keep the choir in the choir loft, a cantor or schola should still be up front to lead the people. When everyone is singing, the focus should be on the leader of that singing, not on the priest-celebrant, the lector or the windows. In order to work effectively, it is important that you claim your position.

Once you take your position in the front of the church, it is important to remember that everyone can see you. You are not only a source of leadership, you also are a potential source of distraction. Therefore you also can and should be a visible source of good example. Your own full participation and attention to the celebration is an important sign. Have yourself well organized so that changing music pages and other chores do not distract from the rest of the celebration.

Few things are more disturbing to people in a church than a musician who looks bored or is just "hanging around" waiting to play the next song. While you lead the congregation, be careful of your facial expressions. Smiles and frowns both communicate a lot to people. Often musicians make a face when they make mistakes. People may never notice your errors if you keep a straight face. You will have to be more attentive and a better communicator if you are in front, but you will be a better leader.

COPYRIGHTS

The daily work of the music minister is directly affected by the fact that much of the music you work with is protected by the Copyright Law. As part of your work, you may wish to make copies of music for either the other musicians, a choir, or the whole community. You certainly may do such copying or printing, provided that you have obtained permission to do so from the copyright owner and comply with instructions stated by the copyright owner. Whether the permission is granted and the terms of the per-

40

mission are both in the hands of the copyright owner.

The matter of copyright protection for religious music is serious business. The U.S. Bishops have made frequent statements calling for compliance with the law and greater respect for the legal and moral rights of composers and publishers. The publishers themselves have tried to make information about copyright procedures as accessible as possible. One publisher has filed significant lawsuits, demonstrating that this is not a matter to be taken lightly.

Many people have good intentions, but they find the process of paying for copyrighted material to be confusing. The only way to totally eliminate confusion is to buy all copies of music you wish to use. If you consider the option of copying and reprinting to be essential to doing your job, familiarize yourself with the copyright policies of the primary publishers or copyright owners whose music you wish to use. These policies vary, so it is necessary to contact each copyright owner separately. Initially you will want to limit your material to the resources of one, two or three good publishers. This practice will simplify the process of obtaining permissions and will keep costs down.

Frequently, musicians have difficulty in tracking down the sources for music they wish to use. This problem is largely avoided by maintaining a good reference collection of published music. The confusion arises from the proliferation of photocopies which do not contain proper source acknowledgements. A good practice is to work only with music for which you have original published editions. If you need help in tracing songs, contact your diocesan music office for information on how to proceed.

Here are some rules of thumb that help keep copyrights from being a headache:

1) Plan ahead, allowing plenty of time for publishers to process permission requests. Ordinarily, allow at least a month.

2) If you have "sudden" music needs, draw from music whose publisher accommodates your requests most easily.

3) Become as familiar as possible with the rich reperotire of "public domain" music, for which reprint permission is not required.

4) Purchase sufficient supplies of a supplementary songbook, so that good music is readily available, even if this book is not used all the time.

5) If you are compiling a parish hymnal or songbook, do it in a looseleaf style. Not only does this permit later additions, but it also lets you begin using the book much sooner, while you are still waiting for slower permissions to materialize.

6) Be realistic about how much new music your parish can learn and the pace of learning. Perhaps, if permissions are giving you too much consternation, you may be adding new music too fast anyway.

Regardless of the kinds of music resources you help choose for your parish, money must be spent. As music minister, you have two important tasks — "lobbying" as much as possible for a music budget that meets the parish needs, and then serving as a responsible steward for that budget, making prudent, worthwhile choices.

V.
Continuing to Grow in Your Ministry

This book provides a collection of information and ideas to help you begin in the ministry of music. Once you make the beginning, you must continue to grow in your ability and your ministry. Never stop learning, refining your musical skills, enriching your repertoire, understanding your ministry more fully and deeply.

PLANS FOR GROWTH

Reflection, Feeback and Evaluation

The best way to learn is through your experiences. To fully use your experiences as a source of growth, however, you must develop a system that helps you do this in an organized manner.

At the end of each season in the church year, take time to personally reflect on how you did. Make notes on what you did well and what you would do differently, and save these notes for future use. In addition, choose one time a year for a major self-evaluation. This need not be shared with anyone, so try to be honest. Following are some general questions to help you in your reflections:

☐ Have you been satisfied with your musical performances?

☐ Did you come to the celebrations really prepared?

☐ Has your music been liturgically appropriate?

☐ Has it helped people to pray?

☐ Are you able to work well with the priests?

☐ Do you have good communication with other people in your parish who also work with the worship program?

☐ Do you have a repertoire of music that adequately meets the needs of your community?

☐ Are you an effective leader of the whole community?

☐ Are you an effective leader of your choir, other musicians?

Feedback from other people can be very important. Many times, the difference between a good celebration and a poor one is in little details that you may never notice. Be open to what you hear from other people, and seek out their impressions and observations informally or through an occasional survey. You need not agree with every opinion, but you should try to learn from them all.

Once a year try to meet with your pastor and other members of the parish to evaluate how you have done. This evaluation need not be a threatening situation for you, in which your job depends on the outcome. It should be an opportunity for you to meet with others who are interested in your growth as well as in the growth of the parish. A good way to structure such a meeting is for you to give an evaluation of yourself as a minister during the past year. Then let them respond and add their own observations and recommendations.

After concluding an evaluation you should make some commitments for growth during the upcoming year. For example, you may decide you need to read more about the theology of worship, or expand your repertoire of psalms, advance your instrumental techniques, or attend a workshop on prayer. Your resolutions need not be shared with others, if you prefer, but write them down to check on yourself.

Musical Training

If you are to continue to grow as a minister of music, it is important to grow as a musician. There is always some music you would like to use that is just beyond your ability. Use your limits as an incentive to practice or to take some lessons. If you are near a college campus, there is also the possibility of taking additional courses on music theory or arranging.

Reading — Books and Periodicals

Continue beyond this introductory booklet in your reading. The Appendix lists some useful books and periodicals. By all means, the heart of the "reading" phase of your ministry education should be **Music in Catholic Worship**, produced by the U.S. Bishops' Committee on the Liturgy and available in a variety of editions.

Workshops

Good workshops on music and worship are continually offered, both locally and nationally. At least once a year, try to attend some kind of workshop or seminar that will help you be a better minister of music. These activities not only give you good information but also provide you with chances to meet other people facing problems similar to your own. Getting out of your parish and sharing ideas with colleagues gives you a useful perspective on your own work.

A minister of music needs skills and qualities other than musical ones. When you look for workshops to attend, consider topics other than liturgy and music. You might profit more from a weekend on prayer or a conference on leadership skills. Consider seminars on sacraments and scripture study as well. You may also consider making a retreat. You will be a better minister if you nourish your personal and spiritual life.

CONCLUSION

Sing the words and tunes of the psalms and hymns when you are together, and go on singing and chanting to the Lord in your hearts, so that always and everywhere you are giving thanks to God in the name of our Lord Jesus Christ.
Ephesians 5:19-20

Continuing
to
Grow
in
Your
Ministry

APPENDIX
More To Read — A Bibliography

BOOKS

Following are selected books and booklets considered helpful to the parish minister of music. In addition to these titles specifically oriented to worship in the parish, be open to further reading in Scripture, spirituality, music in general, and leadership skills.

Bishops' Committee on the Liturgy
Music in Catholic Worship
(Washington, D.C., United States Catholic Conference, 1972)
Also included in PAA's **Sourcebook for Parish Musicians**

Rev. William Bauman
The Ministry of Music
(Washington, D.C., The Liturgical Conference, 1975)

Lucien Deiss
Spirit and Song of the New Liturgy
(Cincinnati, Ohio & Chicago, Illinois, World Library Publications, 1971).

Michael Gilligan
How To Prepare Mass
(Oak Park, Illinois, American Catholic Press, 1971)

Rev. Edward Gutfreund
With Lyre, Harp . . . and a Flatpick: The Folk Musician at Worship
(Phoenix, Arizona, North American Liturgy Resources, 1974).

Bernard Huijbers
The Performing Audience
(Phoenix, Arizona, North American Liturgy Resources, 1972)

Dan F. Onley
Producing and Maintaining Parish Worship Aids: A Handbook
(Glendale, Arizona, Pastoral Arts Associates of North America, 1978).

PAA
Sourcebook for Parish Musicians (Looseleaf Manual with revision service)
(Glendale, Arizona, Pastoral Arts Associates of North America, 1978).

Virginia Sloyan, ed.
Liturgy Committee Handbook
(Washington, D.C., The Liturgical Conference, 1972).

Books, cont.

Eugene A. Walsh, S.S.
Guidelines For Effective Worship
(Phoenix, Arizona, North American Liturgy Resources, 1974).

Eugene A. Walsh, S.S.
The Theology of Celebration and
The Ministry of the Celebrating Community
(Glendale, Arizona, Pastoral Arts Associates of North America, 1977).

Eugene A. Walsh, S.S.
Practical Suggestions For Celebrating Sunday Mass
(Glendale, Arizona, Pastoral Arts Associates of North America, 1978).

Joe Wise
The Body at Liturgy
(Glendale, Arizona, Pastoral Arts Associates of North America, 1972,78).
Originally published by North American Liturgy Resources.

PERIODICALS

Aim ("Aids In Ministry")
(The J. S. Paluch Company and World Library Publications, Chicago).
Free to parish priests, nominal subscription cost to others.
Quarterly.

Hosanna
(North American Liturgy Resources, Phoenix, Arizona)
Free to all who request it; occasional.

Liturgy
(The Liturgical Conference, Washington, D.C.)
Subscription-membership. Monthly.

Modern Liturgy
(Resource Publications, Box 444, Saratoga, California 95070)
Monthly subscription.

PAA Monthly Reporter
(Pastoral Arts Associates of North America, Glendale, Arizona)
Nominal subscription cost, monthly.

Pastoral Music
(National Association of Pastoral Musicians, Washington, D.C.)
Every other month, subscription or membership.

Continuing
to
Grow
in
Your
Ministry